THE

1031

HANDBOOK

Bettye J. Matthews, CPA

ISBN: 0-9725361-0-8

Author: Bettye J. Matthews
Publisher: Bettye J. Matthews

Forward

I have witnessed many "cookie cutter" seminars, training sessions dispensing recipes for exchanging investment real estate. But what happens when the ingredients for the recipe change or are not available? What do these seminars teach about substituting ingredients? Nothing.

In our experience, most Exchangers (taxpayers) begin with questions such as - what if..........., but then what...........? But in my case...........? You get the picture.

All properties for sale and purchase are not created equal. There are differences in structure, order and disorder. Ownership and title differences, shared ownerships, tenants-in-common, joint partnerships, and corporate properties all of which may, in part, combine to make each exchange unique.

Investors need a starting point. And this handbook is just what the doctor ordered. The basic principles are revealed quickly to both new investors and those seasoned veterans in need of a quick review.

The IRS has established a "safe harbor" for both the standard forward and reverse exchanges. However, if you never untie your boat and venture out into and beyond the safe harbor you may never know how many opportunities exist.

If we always seek out the perfect unchallengeable path many good and fair exchanges can be missed.

By investing your time in this little big book [sic] you will open opportunities to real estate investment that you may not have considered.

For example, deferring capital gain tax and putting profit to work buying more investment property or buying that special property first to get it off the market and exchanging later. And consider using profit to leverage even more investment property.

Today's stock market presents an intimidating environment for investors. Many are now turning to real estate to produce the highest and best use of their investment dollars in the foreseeable future.

Now for the good news. In a very real sense this handbook has been a labor of love because Bettye Matthews loves to teach. Bettye Matthews, CPA, developed a course on the "Effect of Taxation on Real Estate" while lecturing at the University of Maryland, University College, at College Park.

During this period, she helped hundreds of licensed real estate brokers learn how to improve their transactions.

It was a natural progression that brings Ms. Matthews, this handbook and you together. Whether you are a real estate investor or thinking of becoming one, this is the place to start.

Warren R. Matthews,
Husband

Mr. & Ms. Matthews will celebrate their 41st wedding anniversary in October 2003. They have two married daughters and three grandchildren.

Table of Contents

Frequently Asked Questions

Appendices

Case Studies - Go Figure

Mr. Spencer's Calculated Decisions
Getting the information
Case I
Case II

Court Cases

But, what have the courts had to say?

Acknowledgments

I want to thank Arlene LaStella of Dunn Title Company in Naples, Florida who was an accounting and tax client. One day she asked me: "Hey Bets, what do you know about 1031 exchanges"?

Can you imagine trading and getting........
New Amsterdam for Beads and Blankets?

Most of us heard the story of Petr Stuyvesant purchasing Manhattan Island from the local Indians for some beads and blankets when we were in Elementary School. Money didn't change hands and so far as dealing with the North American Indian in the 16th Century, money had no value, things had value.

America continued to move on a barter type system for many years, especially in the Northwest Territory where animal pelts were the primary objects of value.   Trappers trapped, middlemen traded food, blankets, guns etc with the trapper and eventually sold the pelts to a furrier who made coats, hats and boots from the animal pelts.

We humans have been trading things for a long time. Until the middle of the 1960's trading meant that you had to find someone who wanted what you had. Then, you had to convince them to find someone who had something you wanted, arrange for a three-way trade or acquire it themselves and then trade with you. This was a long and difficult task which often became unmanageable as our population grew and technological development broadened the list of things we want.

Code section 1031 has it beginnings in the Revenue Act of 1921. Old code section 202 provided for the exchange of property and the non-recognition of gain or loss. It seems that exchanges, at the time, were thought to involve only simultaneous transfers of property. The code section allowed for the deferral of all tax consequences if the taxpayer traded property (personal or real) with another person. Tax treatment under this law is mandatory so you want to be careful how the exchange is treated if you have a loss on the disposition of the property.

Essentially, the law was thought to require traders exchange title in a simultaneous recording of new ownership. Where legal title is a matter of public record, (i.e. land, automobiles, boats etc.) an attorney or closing agent is required to make sure that title (ownership) passed to the respective traders and was recorded in the public records. If other property or cash is used to equalize the value of the two sides offerings, then the other property or cash becomes "boot" and is probably taxable.

The primary rule that **MUST** be met for like-kind exchanges (whether personal property or real property) is that the property must be used in a trade or business or held for investment. In the case of personal property, the question of like-kind is easier to answer (usually). The property is used in a trade or business and it is traded for property used in a trade or business.

Personal property held for investment does exist. It could be gem stones, coins, stamps. They are sometimes traded. A word of warning, a clear understanding of court decisions regarding these types of trades must be obtained before entering such an exchange. (See **Appendix A and B**)

What Really Happens in an Exchange!

The exchange process is really a basis substitution. The basis in the property you traded away becomes the basis in the property you received. You cannot have a basis greater than the fair market value of the property you received. If you receive property of greater value than you gave up, then a basis adjustment may be allowed depending on whether you gave other property or cash as "boot".

An Example:

Relinquished Property

Selling Price	$125,000.
Tax Basis	43,000.
Gain (Profit)	$ 82,000.

Replacement Property

Purchase Price	$150,000.
Basis Old	43,000.
Increased Price	25,000.
Basis New	68,000.
Gain (Profit) New	$ 82,000.

Notice how the basis in the relinquished property is substituted with adjustments as the basis in the new property. This allows the profit you accumulated while you owned the property to be transferred to the replacement property.

Is it Boot or Booty??

In case you are wondering about this word "boot", it appears to have several possible origins. One is that it  comes from the days of sieges and piracy when soldiers and pirates received "extra value" for their hard work in the form of whatever booty they could find, steal or extract from their victims.

A second origin and perhaps more realistic and certainly less romantic is that boot represents throwaway property sort of like "one man's trash is another man's treasure". This other property would be used as an equalizer for a deal where the giver "throws it in to boot" and the receiver gets to "boot around a bit".

Like Kind is not necessarily "Same Kind"

There is great detail within the law and the regulations about what like-kind is and isn't. When trading personal property like automobiles, boats, tools, furniture, equipment etc. the term becomes more exacting and similar use plays an important part.

To determine like-kind for personal property, you must look to the Standard Industrial Code (SIC) for just how similar the use has to be. When trading real property (real estate) the lines are a lot less fuzzy.

In real estate, what would be property used in a trade or business? An auto repair business that owns the building in which it operates would qualify as property used in a trade or business. Some rental properties qualify as a trade or business if it is rented to transient travelers such as the case with a hotel or motel.

Single Family Housing

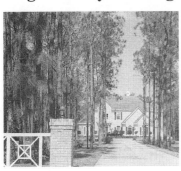

Rental Units

Pasture Land

Agricultural Land

Condominiums

Office Complexes

Wooded Land

In Summary
All of these types of Real Estate are
interchangeable with each other.

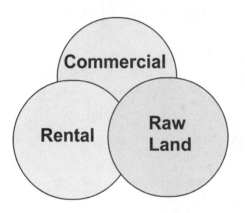

NOTE:
If exchanging a depreciable asset for a non-depreciable asset (land with building for raw land) depreciation recapture may be required.

Any of these investment properties can be traded for any other investment property. It does not have to be the same or even similar use.

The real estate only has to be investment property in the hands of the taxpayer.

However, you cannot trade a property for improvements to be made on other property *you already own*. Many investors want to build a rental dwelling on property they already own.

Their desire is to exchange a property and use the proceeds to build improvements on a vacant lot they already own. *This does not meet the requirements of a like-kind exchange.*

We have to look to another section of the Income Tax Law (Section 1033) for an explanation of why this will not be acceptable. Section 1033 deals with involuntary conversions of property to money.

The section allows for tax deferral on property sold under condemnation or threat of condemnation and for property destroyed by fire, theft or other disaster. Some very special treatment is allowed under these circumstances that permit the taxpayer time (up to two years) to replace or rebuild property lost or damaged due to circumstances beyond their control.

The caveat when dealing with real estate is that you must replace dirt with dirt.

Land lost to condemnation must be replaced with other land. When applying the "dirt for dirt" rule, trading land for an improvement on other land you already own does not qualify.

The law and the regulations are clear on other kinds of property that will not qualify for like-kind treatment. Among them are:

✓ Inventory or other stock in trade
✓ Stocks, bonds or notes
✓ Other securities or evidences
   of indebtedness or interest
✓ Interests in a partnership
✓ Certificates of Trust or Beneficial
   Interests
✓ Choses in action

Trailblazers of a New Frontier in Real Estate

In July, 1967, the Starker Family (father, son and daughter-in-law) entered into an agreement to trade timberland they owned jointly to Crown Zellerbach for other land to be identified and transferred to them within 5 years. Crown Zellerbach agreed to pay cash for any land that was not transferred to the Starkers at the end of 5 years. Furthermore, Crown Zellerbach agreed to credit the Starkers' accounts with a growth factor of 6% at the end of each year.

At the time, the Starkers didn't know which parcels of land they wanted to acquire, but they did know the location of the parcels would be in Oregon or Washington State. The son, Bruce, and his wife, Elizabeth, located their replacement property in just four months. Crown Zellerbach purchased that property and transferred it to the younger Starkers, thus closing their portion of the exchange. T. J. Starker (the father) took nearly two years to identify and acquire 12 parcels of land he wished to receive. At the time, there was nothing within the tax law that specifically prohibited this type of transaction.

When the exchange was complete, the Starkers filed their tax returns reporting the exchange transaction and deferring all gain. The Internal Revenue Service disagreed with their interpretation of §1031 and issued notices of deficiency and requested payment of taxes on what the IRS considered to be the sale of land. Both Starker families paid the deficiency and filed for refund claims. They then filed suit to recover their money.

The son and his wife's case was heard first (Starker I). In this instance the court agreed with the Starkers and found for them. The IRS appealed the decision but later withdrew their appeal allowing the decision to stand.

The father's case (Starker II) was next. The legal maneuvering on each side was remarkable. The same Judge heard Starker II as had heard Starker I. Amazingly, the Judge now found for the IRS and believed he had erred in finding in favor of Starker I in the earlier case. The same defenses and arguments were used as in the earlier case.

Both cases found their way to the appellate court system. Eventually, the Starker transaction with Crown Zellerbach became the first delayed exchange transaction the Internal Revenue Service was unable to characterize as a sale. The cases reached their conclusion in 1977.

By 1991, the Internal Revenue Service was successful in getting Congress to change the law.

While Taxpayers may still trade properties without involving an intermediary. They can engage attorneys and close on their properties in a simultaneous recording of title change by two or more parties sitting at the same settlement table. Congress created the "safe harbor" in 1991, it has made exchanging property much easer for everyone.

Handshakes still work

The Delayed Tax Deferred Exchange and How It Works

These are the true "Starker Exchanges". The taxpayer (exchanger) wishes to change his real estate holdings for other properties that better suit their investment goals. They may want to change the geographical location of the property, or the type of investment property.

Under the current rules, the taxpayer contracts with a realtor, if they wish to use one, to sell the property in question. When an executed contract of sale is complete, the taxpayer should engage an intermediary or other 'safe harbor' to act as the facilitator of the exchange.

There are three other safe harbors available to the taxpayer, however, we believe the intermediary is the easiest method for the exchanger; creates the least problems and requires little effort on the part of the exchanger. *It is important that the contract to sell include a paragraph that states that the seller intends the transaction to be part of a Tax Deferred Exchange and that the purchaser agrees to cooperate.* This paragraph alone clearly establishes the taxpayer's intent to enter into the 1031 exchange process.

We usually insert additional wording that the purchaser will incur no additional cost nor will closing be delayed as a result to the exchange process.

Who can Provide
Intermediary Services?

The law and the regulations are written in such a manner that anyone can be an intermediary. A Qualified Intermediary is merely a person who is not a disqualified person.

The law is very specific on who a disqualified person is. Generally a disqualified person is any person that has acted as an agent of the taxpayer at anytime in the 24 months prior to the beginning of the exchange period.

Typically, disqualified persons are:

- ✓ The taxpayer
- ✓ Family members
- ✓ Employees
- ✓ Attorney
- ✓ Accountant or Tax Preparer of the taxpayer
- ✓ Investment Broker or Banker of the tax- payer
- ✓ Realtor® or Real Estate Agent of the taxpayer or any corporation, partnership or other entity in which the taxpayer/s has a 10% or greater share interest.

A disqualified person is not allowed to act as an escrow agent and cannot receive an identification of replacement property.

The reason great care must be taken to avoid involving a disqualified person is the issue of *constructive receipt.*

Our experience indicates that the intermediary should have detailed knowledge of the workings of §1031 including enough experience to foresee potential problem areas.

Therefore, we believe a qualified intermediary who can perform well for you should have an excellent knowledge of §1031 and be a professional in either the legal or tax accounting field.

Qualified Intermediary

Seller or Exchanger

Buyer Or Exchanger

What is Constructive Receipt?

Constructive receipt occurs when you have dominion and control over the proceeds from the sale of the relinquished property. This is such a touchy subject, the exchange agreement should state unequivocally that you have no control or access to the funds. You may not pledge them as collateral on an unrelated financial matter.

In a recent case, the IRS found that a taxpayer had constructive receipt of his replacement property even though he had used an accommodator for the acquisition. He purchased the property with a mortgage, but failed to include the accommodator on the mortgage as an additional borrower.

Great care must be taken to avoid constructive receipt of the funds in a forward exchange or the replacement property in a reverse exchange.

The Exchange Process

Generally, the exchanger should begin looking for their replacement property immediately upon the decision to sell the investment property they own. It may not be necessary to pin down a specific parcel, but the general location and type of real estate should be established early on in the process.

The intermediary will provide the exchanger with an exchange agreement, which sets out the terms of their contract (agreement). Some important components included in the agreement:

1) The agreement provides for the assignment of both the sale and purchase agreements (contracts).

2) Limits the exchangers access to the proceeds of the sale of the relinquished property. This includes the ability to pledge the proceeds as collateral in an unrelated transaction.

3) Who receives the Growth Factor (interest) on the sale proceeds while in the hands of the intermediary.

4) Provides for the identification of replacement property, the possible revocation and re-identification of other replacement property.

5) Under what circumstances the exchanger will gain access to the proceeds in the event the exchange does not complete itself or if there are excess proceeds.

6) Method of deeding from the exchanger to the intermediary and from the intermediary to the purchaser. A Direct Deed.

7) Responsibilities of the exchanger.

8) Duties of the intermediary.

9) Assumption of Risk clause.

10) Independent status of Intermediary; that an agency relationship does not exist and that the taxpayer (exchanger) has sought their own legal and tax advice.

The money is held by the intermediary

The intermediary will also provide an assignment of the sale contract in which the exchanger assigns their interest in the contract to the intermediary for the purpose of effecting a Section 1031 exchange. As part of the assignment process, a *notice of assignment* is also prepared which is to be signed by the exchanger. The notice is provided to the purchaser of the property and their signature requested as is required by the Internal Revenue Code.

Most of the time, these documents are signed just prior to the property transfer at closing.

Speaking of closing, the intermediary should also provide the closing officer a set of instructions describing the closing process and the method of deeding. In a forward "Starker" exchange a direct deed is used. The term is used in this manner because the exchange agreement and the closing instructions specifically require such a deed but stipulate that the deed will be treated as if deeded from the exchanger to the intermediary and from the intermediary to the purchaser.

The closing instructions usually require the closing officer to secure signatures on the exchange agreement, assignment(s) and notice(s) of assignment prior to the actual closing on the property transfer. This is because the exchange process must begin prior to the property transfer.

In addition to the deeding information, the closing instructions will contain information on how the settlement statement is to be worded. The intermediary is to be shown as an additional seller and the proceeds of sale must go to the intermediary. The instructions will also give direction for forwarding the proceeds to the intermediary.

The exchange period which can run a maximum of 180 days begins on the date of the first transfer of property.

☛The Identification period is imbedded within the Exchange Period

☛The identification period which runs concurrently with the exchange period has a maximum duration of 45 days.

☛Both periods end at midnight on the 180th or 45th day whichever applies.

☛Neither the exchange period or the identification period qualify for an extension of time. Don't bother to ask.

To Illustrate:

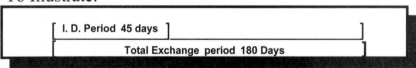

[I. D. Period 45 days]

Total Exchange period 180 Days

Plan Ahead

and your exchange will be free
of worry and frustrations.

To Whom May I Sell My Property?

You can sell your relinquished property to anyone you choose who is a qualified buyer and will follow through with actual closing and transfer of title.

However, if you contract to sell to or buy from a related party, family member, there are restrictions regarding what the family member may do with the property. Remember, in the hands of the purchaser, use is not an issue but when the purchaser is a family member, the property cannot be sold for the 24 month period following the transaction. If it is sold the Internal Revenue Service may challenge the exchange and declare it a sale and thus taxable.

To follow up on this, the Internal Revenue Service requires the purchaser and or seller as well as the exchanger to file form 8824 (like-kind exchanges) with the Internal Revenue Service for the 2 year period subsequent to the exchange year as well as for the exchange year.

A related person is any person related to you within the definition described in the tax law.

Generally this includes your spouse, brother, sister or parent of you or your spouse, your children and grandchildren, foster children, adopted children, nieces or nephews, aunts or uncles and any other person with a direct ancestral or descendent relationship to you. It also includes any entity in which the exchanger (taxpayer) holds a 10% or greater interest.

How do I Identify my Replacement Property?

As unambiguously as possible. Usually the legal description is best but often the mailing address will suffice. Problems with identification begin when large tracts of land are purchased. In this case, the legal description is probably the only unambiguous identification.

You can revoke your identification at any time during the identification period. However, whatever property that is identified as of midnight on the 45th day of the exchange period is the only property that will be considered like-kind for replacement purposes.

How Many Properties May I Identify?

You may identify three (3) properties without regard to the aggregate value of the properties. You may purchase any one property or you may purchase all of the properties.

Example #1:

You relinquish property valued at $150,000.00
You identify 3 properties:
1 valued at $150,000.00
1 valued at $175,000.00
1 valued at $190,000.00
You may close on any of the properties you have identified.

If you identify more than three (3) properties, there is a second tier of rules to be used to determine if the property you receive will be treated as like-kind. This is called the 200% rule. It means that the aggregate (total) value of all of the property you identify cannot be greater than 200% of the aggregate value of the property you relinquished or simply put, twice its value.

If you have failed to identify any property or if your identification is inappropriate, you will only be able to receive your proceeds if the exchange agreement specifically says you may have access to the proceeds under certain circumstances and clearly defines those circumstances.

Example #2:

> You relinquish property valued at $150,000.00
> You identify 5 properties:
> 1 valued at $25,000.00
> 1 valued at $30,000.00
> 1 valued at $35,000.00
> 1 valued at $60,000.00
> 1 valued at $150,000.00

You may close on any combination of the identified properties. Of course, if you fail to close on at least $150,000.00 of value you may be subject to tax.

Finally, even if you exceed the 200% rule there is a third tier at which the property you acquire can still be considered like-kind. This rule is referred to as the 95% rule and is generally a tough standard to meet. This rule requires that you close on and actually acquire 95% of the aggregate value of the property you have identified. To meet this level, be prepared to provide "new" money or to seriously leverage the acquired property.

Example #3:

You relinquish property valued at $150,000.00

You identify multiple properties which exceed both the 3 property rule and the 200% rule.

You identify:
1 property at $125,000.00
1 property at $150,000.00
1 property at $160,000.00
1 property at $100,000.00

There are 4 identified properties whose aggregate value is $535,000.00. In order to have any of your replacement property considered like-kind, you will have to actually acquire $413,250.00 or 95% of the aggregate value. This is a unique situation but very real. In this situation the only property that is not required to be purchased is property #4. Because the 95% rule is in effect, you would have to spend $435,000.00 on replacement property to protect the gain on the $150,000.00 sale from being taxed.

A couple of words of caution when identifying property that is not under contract. First, if your prospective seller becomes aware that you have identified his property as replacement property and the identification period has ended, don't be surprised if your ability to negotiate becomes very limited.

Second, the Internal Revenue Service does not recognize an inability to negotiate an executable contract as sufficient reason to release funds to the exchanger prior to the 180th day unless the exchange agreement stipulates such a release of funds.

Once the property to be relinquished is transferred to the purchaser, you are free to close on the property you intend to acquire any time in the next 180 days.

When the exchanger has an executed contract to purchase replacement property, the same procedure is followed as when the sale agreement was executed. Provide a copy of the purchase contract to the intermediary who will, in turn, provide the required assignment, notice of assignment and closing instructions to the closing officer.

It is important to keep in mind for exchanges whose exchange period began late in the calendar year and can reasonably be expected to extend beyond April 15 (the due date of the tax year in which the exchange period began). Do not file your tax return for the year the exchange period began until the replacement property has been received.

If it is your desire to complete the exchange, you must file for an automatic extension of the filing date. This does not extend the due date for paying whatever taxes may be due.

If you mistakenly file the tax return, the exchange period will have ended on the date of filing and any property you receive after the filing date will not be considered like-kind. Essentially, the transaction that relinquished property becomes a sale and taxes may be due.

Don't file that tax return until the exchange is complete.
The entire exchange must be reported in the same tax year.

Can I Spend More for my Replacement Property?

Indeed, in order to defer all proposed capital gain tax you must replace your property with property of equal or greater value. So if you sell for $100,000 you should replace with a property you purchase for $100,000 or more. Closing costs produce adjustments in basis but are not necessarily deducted from the selling price to produce a net selling price. Sales commission is the only exception in calculating how much must be spent to defer all taxes.

So spending more is never a problem, spending less could cause capital gain to be recognized on the difference in the two values.

Earlier, we discussed 'boot' and described it as other property or cash that is given and or taken during the exchange process. The Internal Revenue Service considers mortgages to be 'boot'. Therefore, if a mortgage exists on the property being relinquished, then, to defer all capital gain tax a purchase money mortgage of the same or greater value must be in place at the time the replacement property is acquired.

An Important Lesson to Remember

Selling Price ≤ Purchase Price

Mortgage Relieved ≤ Mortgage Acquired

Relinquished Equity ≤ Replacement Equity

≤ means less than or equal to

The taxpayers economic condition cannot be improved upon as a direct result of the exchange.

The Reverse Exchange - How it Works

The reverse exchange works very much the same as the forward exchange. There are some subtle but very important differences.

1) You close on the replacement property first.

2) Instead of an Intermediary, you use a qualified accommodator. It is generally the same person or company.

3) Instead of an Exchange Agreement, you use a Qualified Accommodation Agreement.

The contracts to purchase and sell must still be assigned to the accommodator who will prepare notices of assignment and closing instructions for the closing agents.

You still have only 45 days to identify the property you intend to relinquish. Usually this is not a problem but it is important that the qualified accommodation agreement clearly and unambiguously identify the relinquished property. If for some reason you wish to change your identification, you may within the first 45 days of the exchange period.

You also have 180 days to complete the exchange. Failure to complete the exchange within 180 days will result in your owning two properties, neither of which will qualify as like-kind property for each other.

As a practical matter, the exchanger must be prepared to lend the Qualified Accommodator whatever funds are necessary to close on the purchase. The Accommodation Agreement usually includes language about this loan and that the exchanger will provide the needed funds. This loan is repaid at the time of closing on the relinquished property and the replacement property is traded for the relinquished property.

One very significant difference, and one that makes the reverse exchange considerably more expensive, is that the Qualified Accommodator becomes the titleholder of the replacement property until the relinquished property transaction is closed. Usually at the time of the closing of the relinquished property and in a simultaneous closing the Qualified Accommodator will transfer title of the replacement property to the exchanger.

Because the Internal Revenue Service requires that this transfer be for value, a quit claim deed will not meet the criteria. A full real estate closing must take place. Usually this means additional documentary stamps and possibly additional title insurance showing the exchanger as the titleholder and the insured.

It is not unusual for the Qualified Accommodator

to charge a higher fee for the reverse exchange because there is exposure to liability as a result of being the titleholder. Most Qualified Accommodators will establish separate corporations or LLCs for the purpose of holding title in reverse exchanges.

Another cost, though hidden, with the reverse exchange is that the proceeds of sale earn no interest in this type of exchange since there is a simultaneous transfer of the replacement property for the relinquished property. The Qualified Accommodator repays the loan advanced by the exchanger with the proceeds of the relinquished property.

Why Consider a Reverse Exchange?

There are several reasons you might want to consider a reverse exchange. First, you found the property you want to acquire. The price is right and it won't be on the market long. Your long term investment strategy heavily favors this property and the seller wants a quick closing.

Example:

You found a property that will fit your investment goals that is ½ the price of the single family rental property you wish to relinquish. The new property is a 3½ story house that can be converted into three 2-bedroom apartments and 2 studios. This will go a long way toward the retirement nest egg. And the rents will more than meet your immediate requirement for a positive cash flow.

Another reason, the property you want is real cheap but needs work to make it rentable. This is a perfect way to take advantage of the reverse exchange.

You can arrange to purchase the property through a Qualified Accommodator. The Accommodation Agreement can include a clause regarding renovations and allow you to manage the property during the exchange period. You must supply the funds for the renovations. The Accommodator pays the renovation costs from the funds you provide.

The Accommodation Agreement will usually require a full accounting of revenue and expenses during the exchange period, so be prepared to provide a full detailed report. Should there be any profit during the exchange period, a management fee should more than consume that.

What is nice about the Reverse Improvement Exchange is that the property will transfer to the exchanger at the time the relinquished property is closed and transfer for current value. That value will include the cost of renovations, since those costs were added to the Fair Market Value while the Qualified Accommodator was the titleholder.

In the example used here, the rest of the value needed for the exchange to qualify for a full deferral can be provided by the renovations that were made by the Qualified Accommodator.

Finally, you'd rather build on a vacant lot - no problem, if--

A similar reason for the reverse exchange is to buy a vacant lot and build. Again the Qualified Accommodator becomes the titleholder of the vacant lot and allows the exchanger to manage the construction of improvements on the lot. It works the same as the Reverse Improvement exchange and transfers to the exchanger at Fair Market Value on the date of transfer.

AND THEN - Sometimes a reverse becomes necessary - you have a contract on your relinquished property and you've signed a contract to purchase the replacement property. Your buyer fails to perform. Yes, you may have legal remedies, and so will the seller of your replacement property if you fail to close on your contract. A reverse can solve the problem, while you look for another buyer for your relinquished property.

There are Two Types of Reverse Exchanges:

Exchange First and Exchange Last

When you determine that a reverse exchange is necessary to meet your investment goals, there is still another decision to make.

Should you deed your current property to the intermediary or should you allow the intermediary to take title to the property you desire to purchase?

The answer lies in the potential liabilities incurred by ownership.

If there are substantial environmental problems with either the property you seek to sell or that which you want to purchase - the accommodator may not want to assume that type of responsibility.

If your mortgage company will not lend on property you do not own, then the exchange last will not be acceptable.

If your purchased property requires a great deal of management, renovation or is involved in a business that evokes the potential for liability issues - the accommodator may not want to assume that type of responsibility.

Finally, the economic situation needs to meet the requirements of the law may be such that one method may be preferable over the other.

Circumstances may determine which type of reverse exchange you use.

Sometimes the relinquished property does not close "on time" and the planned dates between the two closings is very close. It may be that the deeds, title insurance and mortgage commitment are in place for a normal "Starker Type Exchange".

There may not be enough time for the closing agent to prepare new deeds or get new title insurance commitments. Mortgage underwriters don't like sudden changes no matter what the cause. In a case like that an exchange first is the logical solution.

What Happens if the Improvements are not Completed in 180 Days?

This is where the **IF** comes into play. The Internal Revenue Regulations provide for just such a circumstance. If the property is not going to be completed and an occupancy permit is not granted by the 180th day, there is a method provided for a percentage of completion. The Internal Revenue Service will rely on local custom as to the percentage that is complete. So long as the completed improvement (when complete) is substantially the same as that which was identified as replacement property, the percentage actually completed will be considered like-kind property for exchange purposes.

Example:

You identify a vacant lot to be improved with an 1800 sq. ft. single family dwelling having 3 bedrooms and 2 baths with an attached garage all to be fabricated. The lot is valued at $30,000. Improvements are valued at $80,000 for a total of $110,000.

Your relinquished property sells for $85,000. The Qualified Accommodator holds the proceeds of sale until the improvements are completed on the vacant lot. For various reasons, the improvements are not complete and the exchange period is 170 days old.

The builder cannot finish the project in the next 10 days. A decision is made to have the property inspected by the local authorities to determine a percentage complete.

The inspector finds that the building is only 75% complete but that the remaining work will take more than 10 days to complete.

The regulations allow the Qualified Accommodator to transfer the incomplete improved property to the exchanger on the 180th day at 75% of the proposed fair market value when completed. In this case 75% is equal to 100% of the lot's value or $30,000 plus 75% of the improvements value or $60,000 (75% of $80,000). The total is $90,000 and exceeds the value of the relinquished property. All gain on the transfer will be deferred provided all facets of the regulations are met.

Is There Anything Else I Can Do to Make Sure I Meet the 180 Day Rule on a Reverse Construction Exchange?

Another avenue you can investigate is the "build to suit" contract. Sometimes a builder is willing to improve property he wishes to sell under an agreement for sale. If this type of purchase can be negotiated then the exchange period can be fairly well controlled and a reverse exchange can even be avoided.

What are the Mechanics of a Reverse Exchange?

As previously mentioned the intermediary in a reverse exchange is called the Accommodator. Under normal circumstances, the Accommodator will make arrangements to form a Limited Liability Company (LLC) or a Corporation (S or C but usually S) who will serve as the Exchange Accommodation Titleholder (EAT) in the transaction. For liability purposes, it is best that the property being acquired is the only property in which the EAT holds title. The purpose is to limit the exposure of other exchanger's property and at the same time protect your property from any claims arising out of other property owned by the EAT. This is especially true in a case where an environmental impact statement is required or an environmental assessment of hazardous waste is necessary because of previous uses of the property. There may be additional costs incurred for establishing the LLC or the corporation.

What about Tenancy in Common (TICs)?

Earlier, we said that partnership interests were not eligible for like-kind treatment. However, a type of shared ownership is eligible for exchange treatment. The Tenant in Common is a very special type of group ownership. Any member of the group may dispose of their ownership interest and enter into a 1031 Exchange if they desire.

A tenancy in common is different from a partnership for the following reasons:

1)   A legal or defacto partnership is never formed

2)   Earnings and expenses are reported as a pro rata share on the individual owner's tax returns

3)   The group owners never request or receive a taxpayer identification number (TIN) from the Internal Revenue Service

4)   A tax return for the group is never filed with the Internal Revenue Service

5)   The deed to the property lists the owner(s) as tenants in common

One of the most common tenancy-in-common real

estate practices today is the condominium.

The condo association owns the land, buildings and amenities. The individual owners own the interior space including floor coverings, window treatments, appliances, etc. etc. and an undivided interest in the common elements of the condominium association.

Tenancy in Common is a very useful tool for those investors wishing to retire from the real estate management business. The investor may have grown tired of leaky faucet phone calls, collecting rents or dealing with the current tenant/landlord laws. A Tenancy in Common ownership in a large office building could be the relief you have been searching for.

You can exchange your ownership interest in single family rental properties for a tenancy in common in other investment real property.

A group of owners own the building and hire a management company to manage the building. Typically, there would be 1 to ½ dozen tenants in the building, all under long term leases.

Where do you find this dream ownership? Usually a promoter puts this type of deal together.

Generally, this is how it works:

A promoter has purchased a $5 Million office building that has 2 tenants. One tenant has 10 years remaining on their underlying lease and two 10-year options to extend. The other tenant has recently moved in and has 15 years remaining on its lease and has three 5-year options to renew.

The promoter, who is also a management company, wishes to acquire other investors to own the building. Gradually, new investors are found. They purchase a percentage undivided ownership and share in the revenues and expenses for the property to the extent of their ownership share. Normally, the management company will build cash reserves for major repairs or to manage a vacancy period should one of the tenants decide not to renew its lease. These buildings are usually financed with non recourse debt, rents are set at a level which meets all expenses and leaves some profit so the owners receive a return on their investment. Most promoters try to establish an 8% return for their investors. Checks are usually issued monthly and sometimes quarterly.

Another excellent use for the Tenant in Common ownership is as a backup for an existing exchange. Sometimes the exchanger is so intent on acquiring a specific parcel, the 45-day identification period passes without their having named an alternative investment. Tenant in Common ownership can be arranged in a few days even in a few hours. But, if it is not identified as a possible replacement property, it cannot be treated as like-kind. Most Qualified Intermediaries have a working relationship with several promoters of Tenant in Common packages and can refer you to them.

What Happens to my Tax Basis in an Exchange?

As mentioned earlier, the tax basis of the property that is relinquished is carried over as the basis of the replacement property. There are some adjustments to basis that can be made. For instance, if the replacement property cost more than the relinquished property sold for, you may adjust the carryover basis by the additional cost. The basis is also adjusted for the costs of acquisition which are not otherwise deductible. These closing costs could be title insurance, legal fees, search fees, document stamps, etc.

Example:

You contract to sell your relinquished property for $100,000. Your accountant tells you that your tax basis is $42,000. $15,000 of the basis is in non-depreciable land and the remaining $27,000 is the remaining book value on the improvements to the land. Your proposed capital gain is $58,000 ($100,000 - $42,000). The property is unencumbered. You have every reason to consider an exchange.

You locate and identify a property that you negotiate a purchase price of $135,000. You elect to acquire a mortgage for the additional money needed.

In this example the entire capital gain amount is deferred into the replacement property because you purchased for more than you sold and the mortgage you acquired is greater than the mortgage you gave up (zero).

Your new tax basis will have several components:

The Enhanced Improvements will begin to be depreciated using the depreciation guidelines in effect at the time of closing. In 2001, that would mean MACRS over a 39 year period.

Exchanged Land Value		$15,000.
Exchanged Improvements		27,000.
(Book Value)		
Depreciation Allowed or		
Allowable		19,000.
(Not Important in this exchange)		
Enhanced Land Value		7,500.
Enhanced Improvements		27,500.
New Basis:	Land	$22,500.
	Improvements	$54,500.

The land continues to be a non-depreciable asset.

The Exchanged Improvements will continue to be depreciated in the same manner as before. This means that the depreciation rate and years of service remain the same in the new property as in the old property. If the improvements on the new property have a fair market value greater than that of the old property, the difference is depreciated at a new rate.

What Happens to Depreciation on My Relinquished Property?

Depreciation is a characteristic of basis and carries to the replacement property as part of the tax basis. In the previous example we said the $19,000 in depreciation had been allowed over the ownership period of the exchanger. In actuality we were saying that the exchanger had purchased the property for $61,000 and that $19,000 had been depreciated leaving the current tax basis as $42,000.

When a depreciated property is sold the gain on the sale has two components; appreciated gain and depreciated gain. Under the current tax code, depreciated gain is taxed at 25% and appreciated gain is taxed at a maximum of 20%.

When a taxpayer enters an exchange and replaces the relinquished property with a property of less value, any difference could be subject to tax, and if it is taxed, it will be at the highest rate first. This means that depreciation gain will be taxed first (depreciation recapture) and appreciation gain will be taxed only when all depreciation gain has been exhausted.

Keep in mind, however, depreciation must be recaptured if the replacement property is non-depreciable raw land.

What About my Holding Period on the Relinquished Property?

The holding period is another characteristic of basis. It carries over to the new property along with the substituted basis. In the above example, suppose the exchanger purchased the $61,000 property just 14 years prior to the date he closed on the replacement property. With respect to the $61,000 initial investment in the asset, the 14 years of ownership attached to that portion of the replacement property. As to the enhanced value of the replacement property, the holding period begins anew. The additional $35,000 paid for the new property establishes its own holding period and will be taxed accordingly when disposed of.

If you have held the property you wish to relinquish less than two years, be sure to consult with your tax professional regarding the exchange. There is considerable disagreement regarding exchanges of real property held for less than two years.

The Internal Revenue Code and the regulations are silent with regards to how long you must hold the property. However, it is clear that foreigners exchanging personal property are only required to consider the use of the property during their ownership if their ownership is less than two years.

What is Capital Gain?

Capital Gain occurs when you sell a capital asset and realize a profit on the sale. Whether you will be required to recognize the sale as a taxable event will be determined by the circumstances which caused you to convert the asset into cash.

If a government agency (Local, State or Federal) condemned the asset, there are rules which will allow you to replace the asset without having to recognize the sale.

If the asset was destroyed in a natural disaster, there are rules which will allow you to replace the asset without having to recognize the sale.

And if the asset was destroyed by a sudden event which was beyond your control (like fire), there are rules which will allow you to replace the asset without having to recognize the sale.

If you elect to sell your primary residence, there are rules which can offer relief from recognition if your entire gain is less than $250,000 ($500,000 if married filing jointly) and you have owned and used the residence as your primary residence for 2 of the 5 years immediately prior to the sale.

Finally, for investors in real estate there is the like-kind exchange which is available. Using the like-kind exchange allows the taxpayer to delay the realization and therefore the recognition of gain on the sale of a capital asset.

Capital gain can be long-term. This means that you owned the property for a period of time longer than one year. This is where the common phrase, year and a day, is most often heard. Long-term capital gain is currently (2002) taxed at 20%.

Capital gain can also be short term if you owned the property in question for one year or less. Short term capital gain is taxed at whatever the taxpayers prevailing ordinary income rate is for the year of sale.

Frequently

Asked

Questions

(FAQs)

What if I own real estate as an individual and wish to include my spouse on title for the replacement property?

The mechanics of the §1031 Exchange require that the title holder be the same at the end of the exchange as at the beginning. In this case to preserve all of the ability to defer tax on the sale of property, it is recommended that property be purchased having twice the value of that which was relinquished. In order to defer all tax, the exchanger (in this case one member of a married couple) would have to reinvest all of the proceeds in the replacement property. This would necessitate that the exchanger own at least 50% of the replacement property.

Another method, if there is enough time to complete the recording of a deed, would be to put the spouse on the deed of the relinquished property prior to selling the property. Obviously, the more time that passes between the inclusion of the spouse on the deed and the closing date of the sale, the better able the transfer of title will survive inspection.

It is important that the titleholder of the replacement property be the same as the titleholder of the relinquished property. If a corporation owns the real estate, then the corporation is the exchanger.

Can I exchange a Vacation Rental?

It stands to reason that if you own a vacation rental and meet the 14 day or 10% of the rental period that you would be able to exchange a vacation rental. It is clearer if you exchange a vacation rental for a vacation rental but if you follow the rules for investment property it should not be a problem.

However, when your personal use is greater than 14 days or 10% of the rental period you are required to bifurcate the expenses between investment rentals and personal use when reporting the rental income and expense on your annual tax return.

There is no authority that addresses such a situation, but it is believed that with an adequate facts and circumstances approach to the exchange, the exchange would survive an audit by the Internal Revenue Service.

And a Guest House?

I own a home which I use as a personal residence. Connected to that home and on the same plot of land is a guest house which I have rented every year for the last 15 years. I report my revenue and expenses on Schedule E of my form 1040 and take depreciation on the guest house.

Can I use an exchange for the guest house while claiming primary residence exclusion on the main house?

Again, the Internal Revenue Service requires you to bifurcate the common expenses of operating the real estate. You must divide the real estate taxes and other expenses between the two dwelling units.

While there is no authority that addresses this specific situation, it is reasonable that when a facts and circumstances test is applied, the same ratio of basis allotted to the guest house over the 15 year period could be applied to the Fair Market Value of the real estate at the time of sale. In this way a value for the investment property could be established and adequate arguments could be presented that support the guest house portion of the property being eligible for §1031 exchange treatment.

I understand the related party rules as they affect §1031 exchanges, but what if the related party dies?

If either party to a related party exchange dies during the 24 month period immediately following the last transaction in the exchange, the non-recognition clause will not apply.

This means that the exchange will remain intact and the gain continues to be deferred.

The same will apply if either the relinquished or the replacement property is converted to cash through a compulsory or involuntary conversion. Such a conversion will occur if a government takes the property in imminent domain or if the property is destroyed by fire, flood, or other natural disaster.

Can I exchange three properties for only one property? How would it work?

It is perfectly reasonable to exchange three properties for a single property. It is a little more work and the intermediary may charge for the extra work, especially if the relinquished properties are sold to three different purchasers and represent three entirely separate closings.

The time lines are the same; 180 days for the exchange period and 45 days for the identification period. Both periods begin as of the closing of the first property. As to the basis in the new property, it will be the aggregate of the bases of the three properties. Depreciation methods and length of time will remain the same as with the relinquished properties. This can be a bit of a problem but some decent fixed asset software should be able to handle it. Of course, if the replacement property costs more than the aggregate of the relinquished properties selling prices, a fourth depreciation factor will have to be figured into the process.

What about exchanging one property for three properties?

Again, the process remains the same. How the basis in the relinquished property is treated is a little different. In this case, the aggregate value of the replacement properties would be compared to the selling price of the relinquished property and ratios developed.

Each of the replacement properties would assume its proportionate share of the basis. Again depreciation method and length of time remain the same. Any additional price paid for a replacement property would be added to basis but depreciated using acceptable depreciation methods in effect at the time of purchase.

I own two unimproved (vacant) lots. Can I sell one and use the proceeds to build a rental unit on the other?

This is one area that investors would love to see a change in the regulations. You won't find the answer in §1031 of the code but you will find the answer in §1033 regarding condemnations and the deferral of taxes.

The regulations require that "dirt" be exchanged for "dirt". If you sell land and replace it with a dwelling unit on another lot you already own, you have not met the "dirt for dirt" criteria and the replacement property will not be considered like-kind.

Can I sign a contract to purchase my replacement property before my relinquished property sells?

Absolutely!! The time lines the regulations set out are always as of the closing date of the first transaction in an exchange.

Be careful that your closing date is sufficiently far enough in the future so as to not force you into a reverse exchange. There is nothing wrong with a reverse exchange, they are merely more expensive. A little attention to this detail can avoid those added costs.

Can I take back a note on my relinquished property?

The regulations indicate that a security agreement such as a mortgage or a deed of trust is one of the 'safe harbors' from constructive receipt of the proceeds.

However, if you elect to take back a note, make sure it is secured with a mortgage and/or Deed of Trust and that the note cannot be construed as cash or a cash equivalent. It is important that no payments on the note be received by the exchanger during the 180 day exchange period. In making a decision to finance the sale or a part of it, rely on the advice of your attorney or tax preparer.

I've often heard that a leasehold interest of 30 years or more was equivalent to ownership in fee. Does a leasehold of 30 years or more qualify for like-kind exchange treatment?

Yes it does. In fact, if you hold a leasehold interest in increments of 30 years, say like a 99 year lease with 92 years remaining, you may exchange the next 30 year period and regain possession of the leasehold in the 31st year.

There are very few cases where only the proceeds need to be reinvested. The regulations require that the exchanger's economic condition cannot be improved by the exchange.

In order to accomplish this, the fair market value of the replacement property should be equal to or greater than that of the relinquished property.

Your equity in the replacement property should be the same as or less than your equity in the relinquished property. If you had a mortgage on the relinquished property it is usually best to have a mortgage of the same or greater value on the replacement property as well.

How much money must I reinvest?

The rules require that your economic condition not be improved after the exchange is completed. Therefore, reinvesting only the proceeds from the sale may not meet the criteria for a complete deferral. It depends, if you had a mortgage on the property you relinquished, then you should have a mortgage on the property you acquire. By doing this, you avoid mortgage boot and your equity in the new place will be similar to the equity in the old place.

Can I get money out of the exchange to use for other purposes?

Generally no. The proceeds of the sale of the relinquished property go to the intermediary and the intermediary uses those funds to purchase the replacement property. You may have to procure a mortgage in order to provide all the money necessary to close on the replacement property.

During the exchange period, you may not have access to the proceeds at any time.

However, it is possible for you to take money out at the beginning or after the exchange has ended. You can chose to equity finance prior to selling the relinquished or you can refinance the mortgage immediately after closing on the replacement property.

Some tax professionals may encourage you to take a larger mortgage than necessary and take the money at closing. When you do this, the excess funds are returned to you at closing and thought to come to you in the form of borrowed money rather than proceeds on the exchange. This can be a dangerous method for taking money out of the exchange.

You must always keep in mind, that the Internal Revenue Service wants to tax whatever amounts it can and it will be you that must defend your method. Often, the cost of defense is greater than the tax on the amount received. The author's opinion is: **Don't tempt the IRS**. Take some equity financing on the relinquished or equity finance the replacement or if you choose, refinance the mortgage on the replacement.

The important thing to remember, is understand the rules so you can make informed decisions.

Can I use the proceeds to make deposits on the replacement property?

Yes, the funds held by the intermediary can be used to make the good faith deposit as well as additional deposits on the replacement property.

Checks should not be made payable to you but to the escrow agent holding the deposits on the contract. That escrow agent should not be your attorney.

The contract to purchase should stipulate when additional deposits are due. In the case of an additional deposit required in order to extend the closing date on the contract, make sure an addendum is prepared.

How do I report the exchange on my tax return?

For the tax year in which the exchange began, form 8824 (Like-Kind Exchanges) must be included in your tax return.

It is very important that you never file a tax return for the year in which the exchange began until the exchange is completed or the exchange period has expired.

The courts have held on several occasions that tax returns filed when an exchange is incomplete effectively ends the exchange period. Property received after the date the tax return is filed will not be considered like-kind.

If your exchange is not completed by April 15 of the year following the beginning of the exchange period, simply file an automatic extension of time to file. Make sure any taxes that might be due with the extension are timely paid so the extension is valid.

How long must I have owned the property I wish to relinquish?

Section 1031 offers little guidance when searching for an answer to this question. If we look to Section 1221 which describes what a Capital Asset is, we will find information that will tell you the holding period of the relinquished asset is tacked on to the holding period of the replacement property.

Currently, there are differences in opinion among the Qualified Intermediaries, Accommodators and tax preparers. Obviously, the longer you hold the property the better.

It is necessary that you have held the property long enough and in a manner consistent with investment use that the IRS will be unable to claim that you held the property for resale. Holding for resale would indicate that the property might be inventory and remember from earlier on in this handbook, inventory does not qualify for like-kind exchange.

How long must I hold the replacement property?

The answer to this question is as difficult as the last. You should plan to hold the property as long as necessary to show that your intent to enter into an exchange was bonafide. However, there are instances when you have become the new owner of property that someone else wants at any price.

If this should happen, make sure you have not made any indication to anyone that the property is for sale. Don't discuss selling the property with Realtors or even family members.

The offer you receive from the person willing to pay anything to have that piece of property must be unsolicited. In fact, if you accept the offer make sure you get a notarized letter from the buyer that his offer was unsolicited and that he approached you about selling.

There are never any promises that your word will be accepted at face value by the IRS. Always document, and the more the better.

And, as with the relinquished property, the length of time the property is held and its use must be consistent with investment use.

Suppose I have a second home and wish to exchange it?

Second homes which are used personally are not generally eligible for like-kind treatment. However, you can change the use of the property and thereby make it eligible. You can do that by making it clear to colleagues and family members that you no longer intend to use the property for personal use. Follow up on that by contacting a Real Estate Rental Management company and list the property for rent. The rents requested should be fair market value. There should be nothing in the offer to lease that would discourage a potential renter. Whether you offer the property for annual lease or seasonal lease doesn't really matter. **Any fair market value renter is better than none. But please, the one thing you must plan for, is to not use the property for personal use.**

How long you should hold the property after changing its use?

There is no firm period of time to guide you. Only, the longer the better. Make sure you rely on your tax preparer for the best advice for your situation. And, document, document, document. There is no such thing as too much documentation when changing from personal use to investment use.

There is case law (see appendix) that suggests the holding period of converted personal use property could be a little as a few months.

Can I exchange investment property and later convert it to personal use property?

Indeed you can. This seems to be a favorite tool for retirement planning. Most guidelines will indicate that you should continue the investment use for a minimum of two years especially if your plan is to convert its use to personal use.

As with other questions regarding changing the use of property, the longer you maintain the investment use the better your chances of the exchange surviving an audit by the IRS.

There is always the requirement that the taxpayer enter an exchange with the bonafide intent to complete the exchange. Unforeseen changes in circumstances can alter the eventual out come but do not necessarily change your intent.

APPENDICES

Appendix A

Property that <u>Does Not Qualify</u> for Like-Kind Treatment

Foreign Real Estate is not like-kind to United States Real Estate

Primary Residence is not like-kind to Single Family Rental property or any other type of rental property.

Second Home is not like-kind to Single Family Rental property or to Rental Condo property or to any other type of investment property.

Personal use property (Primary residence or second home) is not like-kind to investment property.

Gold Coins are not like kind to bullion or to bullion quality coins.

Land (vacant or not) is not like-kind to an improvement on another parcel of land already owned by the taxpayer.

Appendix B

Property that <u>Does Qualify</u> for Like-Kind Treatment

A rental single family residence is like-kind to a duplex or a quadroplex.

A rental condominium is like-kind to a rental single family residence.

A rental dwelling unit is like-kind to a commercial rental unit.

A vacant lot or land is like-kind to investment rental real estate.

Pasture land or farm land is like-kind to investment rental real estate if you lease the land to a rancher or tenant farmer.

FCC radio licenses are like-kind to FCC television licenses.

Gold Coins of one Nation are not like-kind to those of another Nation.

Appendix C

§1031 Checklist of To-Dos

To defer all Capital Gain and Depreciation Recapture tax, the following MUST be met:

    1) Engage one or more of the 'Safe Harbors' allowed by the IRS.

> Qualified Intermediary
> Qualified Escrow Accounts
> Qualified Trust
> Security or Guarantee Arrangement
> Mortgage, Deed of Trust, or other security interest in property so long as it is not cash or cash equivalents.

    2) Enter into a process that clearly shows your intention to engage in the exchange process.

    3) Identify your replacement property within 45 days of the closing date of your relinquished property.

    4) Take ownership of the replacement property within 180 days of the closing date of your relinquished property.

    5) Value of the property acquired must equal the value of the property relinquished with some very limited adjustments.

6) Value of a mortgage you are relieved of at the transfer of the relinquished property must be replaced with a mortgage of equal or greater value on the replacement property.

7) Do not file a tax return for the year in which the exchange period began until after the exchange or the exchange period is completed.

Remember to get professional help!!

Glossary

§1031 Exchange
A method for exchanging property whereby the exchanger can defer all capital gain taxes if certain rules are met.

Accommodator
In a reverse exchange the Accommodator serves as the unrelated third party that accomplishes the exchange in behalf of the exchanger.

Assignment
A party to a contract gives their contractual rights to another party.

Basis
The unrecovered investment an owner has in the property owned.

Boot
That portion of exchanged goods that do not qualify for like-kind treatment.

Build to Suit
Can be used to stretch the construction period beyond the 180 exchange period by timing the transfer of the relinquished property to within 180 days of the completion of the specified replacement property.

Capital Gain
The portion of an owners equity that results from appreciated value.

Exchange Period
The 180 day period following the first transaction in the exchange process.

Exchange First
In a reverse exchange, the property to be purchased is identified as replacement property and acquired by the exchanger. The relinquished property is parked with the EAT.

Exchange Last
A Reverse Exchange. The identification of the Relinquished property is delayed until after the replacement property is acquired. The replacement property is parked with the EAT.

Forward Exchange
The relinquished property transaction occurs first.

Identification Period
The period within the exchange period that is the first 45 days after the first transaction takes place.

Like-Kind
Refers to properties that are of a similar use in the hands of the owner.

LLC (Limited Liability Company)
A legal entity that can own property and perform services very much like a corporation but whose participants are members rather than shareholders.

Mortgage
An encumbrance on real property that secures a lender's interest in a promissory note.

Parking Transaction
A reverse exchange is commonly referred to as a parking transaction because the replacement property is parked in the name of an Exchange Accommodation Titleholder and transferred to the exchanger at a later date.

Phantom Income
Income that is not realized by the taxpayer but becomes taxable. The most common is interest income imputed on Original Issue Discount Transactions.

Qualified Intermediary
The person or entity that is not disqualified from serving as a qualified intermediary who sells and purchases the exchange benefit for the exchanger.

Relinquished Property
The property being disposed of by the exchanger.

Replacement Property
The property being acquired by the exchanger.

Reverse Exchange
A process whereby the exchanger acquires the replacement property first through an Exchange Accommodation Titleholder.

Safe Harbor
Processes offered within the IRS regulations that are considered safe and will not be questioned by the IRS when followed.

Starker
The family who in the 1960's successfully challenged the exchange rules and completed the first successful delayed exchange.

Tax Basis
The unrecovered cost of an asset. Generally this is cost plus improvements and less depreciation allowed or allowable.

White Knight
This party comes to the rescue of an exchanger whose forward exchange has gone sour and is forced to close on the replacement property before the relinquished transaction is completed.

ALPHABET SOUP

EAT- Exchange Accommodation Titleholder

IRC - Internal Revenue Code. Laws passed by Congress regarding the taxation of persons and the regulations which interpret the law.

IRS - Internal Revenue Service. An agency of the Treasury Department charged with the implementation of tax law and the collection of taxes.

OID - Original Issue Discount. Interest imputed on the face value of a delayed negotiable instrument.

PLR - Private Letter Ruling requested by a taxpayer and issued by the IRS.

QEAA- Qualified Exchange Accommodation Agreement

QI - Qualified Intermediary

QIO - Qualified Indicia of Ownership - Those Burdens and Benefits of ownership that clearly indicate the owner of property.

TAM - Technical Advice Memorandum issued by the IRS

CASE

STUDIES

GO FIGURE

John Spencer's Calculated Decisions

A Case Study -
or two

Getting the information

Acting on it

Case Study I Forward Exchange

How to calculate your tax basis?

John Spencer purchased rental property in 1993 for which he paid $75,000.00 - John made renovations in 1995 totaling $4,500.00. All other changes to the property have been handled as repairs.

PURCHASE PRICE	$75,000.00
+ RENOVATIONS	$ 4,500.00
TOTAL COST	**$79,500.00**
- DEPRECIATION TAKEN	$21,373.20
TAX BASIS	**$58,126.80**

The tax rate on Capital Gain is determined by how long the taxpayer has held the property/investment.

	Your tax Bracket
Short Term < 1 Years	
Long Term > 1 Years	20%

John Spencer discovered that if he sells his rental property he will have to pay 20% of his profit of $58,126.80 ($11,625.36) as a Capital Gain Tax.

How to calculate your Capital Gain?

John Spencer decided to sell the rental property he had purchased in 1993. Using the information developed when he determined his tax basis, the following is an estimate of the Capital Gain John would recognize.

SELLING PRICE	$200,000
COST OF SALE:	
- COMMISSIONS	$ 12,000
- CLOSING	$ 3,000
NET SELLING PRICE	$185,000
LESS THE TAX BASIS	$ 58,126
CAPITAL GAIN	$126,874

How to estimate the tax due?

John Spencer now knows how much Capital Gain he should receive. The next step in determining if an exchange is reasonable, is to compute the estimated tax due if he were to sell the property.

The Capital Gain he calculated is:

$126,874

THE GAIN HAS TWO COMPONENTS:

I.	DEPRECIATION RECAPTURE	$ 21,374
II.	LONG TERM CAPITAL	$105,500
	CALCULATED CAPITAL GAIN	$126,874

Depreciation is recaptured and taxed at 25%. In John's case this is $5,343.50

Long Term Capital Gain is currently taxed at 20%, in John's case this amount is $21,100.

TOTAL ESTIMATED TAX DUE
$26,443.50
(IF THE PROPERTY IS SOLD)

Should John Spencer enter into a Like-Kind Exchange?

Yes, John should seriously consider a 1031 exchange.

For Comparison

An exchange of property in a case similar to John Spencer's would incur exchange fees in the neighborhood of $1,000 - $1,500.

This exchange will produce a reinvestment opportunity of approximately $25,000 otherwise lost to capital gain taxes.

COST OF AN EXCHANGE

Forward 1031 Exchange	$1,000 - $1500.
Sale and Purchase	$25,000 of **LOST** Investment Opportunity

Case Study II   Reverse Exchange

John Spencer's Real Estate Agent has found the perfect property for John to add to his investment portfolio. But, John needs time to sell the property he wants to relinquish. The price is right and it won't be on the market long. This property is just what John has been looking for to move his retirement plans forward. What can John do?

A reverse exchange? Yes! That's what John should consider and it's what his Realtor® should suggest.

This property is a large home that has been divided into three separate apartment units. It needs some renovations before it can produce rent. The property can be purchased for $200,000.

The property John intends to relinquish (sell) in the exchange is valued at $400,000.

John Spencer's calculations will be done in the same way as the forward exchange in Case I.

John needs to determine if this exchange, as presented, will be beneficial.

Calculating Basis in Replacement Property

PURCHASE PRICE REPLACEMENT	$250,000
NET SELLING PRICE RELINQUISHED	$185,000
DIFFERENCE	$ 65,000 POTENTIAL TAX DUE IF NEGATIVE
TAX BASIS IN RELINQUISHED	$ 58,126
NEW TAX BASIS	$123,126
CAPITAL GAIN TRAPPED IN NEW PROPERTY	$126,874

The Next Decision

If John Spencer decides that it is in his best interest to do a reverse exchange one more decision is required. Should he:

Exchange First

John can <u>exchange first</u> by deeding his current property to an intermediary/accommodator **before** purchasing the new property.

- or -

Exchange Last

John can <u>exchange last</u> by lending his accommodator the funds necessary to purchase the new property. The property would be titled in the name of the accommodator until the relinquished property is sold.

The decision John makes here is determined by the circumstances surrounding the transaction. These circumstances are discussed on pages 35 - 39.

COURT

CASES

And the Courts Say.........

Case #1

Bundren v. Commissioner, KTC 2002-97 (10th Cir. 2002)

Summary

The taxpayer had a primary residence which they purchased in 1982 for $183,000 and in the next 10 years made $50,000 in improvements. Therefore, their basis in their primary residence was $223,000. In June of 1994 the taxpayers converted their primary residence into rental property.

In September, 1994, they listed the property for sale for $134,500. In December 1994, they exchanged the property for another investments property. The exchange credit was based on the listed sale price.

The IRS challenged the depreciation deduction on the exchanged property as excessive and the loss claimed on the taxpayers 1996 tax return; the year they sold the exchanged property. The taxpayers and the IRS agreed that the exchange transaction qualified under 26 U.S.C. Section 1031 and that "boot" had been received. The only remaining issue was the carryover basis of the of the converted primary residence to the exchange property.

The Court agreed with the IRS because .....

The basis in the property was its fair market value on the date of conversion. Since the taxpayer listed the property for $134,500 and exchanged it at that value only six months after the conversion, the commissioner (of the IRS) determined that $134,500 was its Fair Market Value on the date of conversion and that the more than $200,000 depreciable basis which was used as the basis in the exchange property was excessive and disallowed the excessive depreciation and the excessive loss reported on the taxpayers tax returns.

Interesting points in this case.....

You can convert your primary residence to rental property

The IRS appeared to be unconcerned about the short holding period as investment property. You may not have to hold the converted investment property for 24 months prior to an exchange

The basis in the converted investment property is your cost or its fair market value on the date of conversion whichever is lower.

Lesson in this case.....

The IRS can and will reach back to examine your carryover basis.

Case #2

Christensen v. Commissioner,
KTC 1999-535 (9th Cir. 1998)

Summary

The taxpayers entered into an exchange in late 1988. Their 1988 tax return was due on April 15, 1989. The taxpayers did not acquire their replacement property prior to the due date of their tax return, failed to request an extension of the April 15 filing dead line, furthermore, they filed a tax return that did not include information regarding the exchange.

The IRS challenged the non-recognition of gain on the exchanged property. The commissioner determined that the transfer of properties did not qualify for like-kind treatment.

The Court agreed with the IRS because ......

Code section 1031(a) (3) (B) (ii) clearly sets the time limit for completing an exchange as 180 days from the first transfer of property or the due date plus granted extensions of the taxpayers tax return for the year in which the exchange began. The taxpayers, filed their 1988 tax return which effectively ended their exchange period. Property received after the exchange period has ended cannot be considered of a like-kind.

Interesting points in this case ....

If your exchange period extends beyond the due date of the tax return for the year in which the exchange began, request an automatic extension of time to file. The automatic extension will reset your due date as August 15 allowing more than enough time to complete any exchange that began prior to January 1.

Lesson in this case.......

Do not file your tax return for the year in which the exchange began until the exchange is complete and you can report the entire transaction.

Case #3
DeCleene v. Commissioner,
115 T.C. 457

Summary

Taxpayer operated his business on property (property A) he owned since 1977. In 1992, the taxpayer purchased an unimproved lot (property B) at another location. In September, 1993, the taxpayer entered into an agreement with another party (X) wherein they agreed that the improved property A was of equal value to the unimproved lot, property B. The taxpayer quit claimed property B to X for a deferred cash consideration of $142,000.

X agreed to build on the lot a structure to the taxpayer's specifications. The taxpayer was responsible for all transaction costs and carrying costs. The construction was financed by a mortgage and a note guaranteed by the taxpayer and was nonrecourse to X. The taxpayer assumed personal liability for the note and mortgage at the time property A was exchanged for property B in it improved state.

The IRS challenged the transactions and determined that actual transaction was a sale of property A to X.

The Court agreed with the IRS because ....

Though this appears to be a reverse exchange, it occurred prior to the issuance of Reg Proc 2000-37 which provides a safe harbor for reverse exchanges. Therefore Rev Proc 2000-37 does not apply.

The taxpayer did not locate and simply identify property B as potential replacement property for property A. The taxpayer purchased it without the participation of an exchange facilitator a year or more prior to his intention to build and occupy. He then transferred title, subject to a reacquisition agreement, and at the same time obligated himself to relinquish property A.

The Court looked to the 3 month ownership period of property B by X to determine if X had received all of the benefits and burdens of ownership. The Court determined that X acquired no equity interest in property B, it made no economic outlay to acquire property B, it was not at risk to any extent because it's obligation and security interest was nonrecourse. X was only obligated to reconvey the improved property B to the taxpayer pursuant to a prearrangement the taxpayer was obligated to take and pay for.

The Court determined that the real economic transaction occurred when the taxpayer transferred title of property A to X in exchange for $142,400 which actually occurred at the time of the 'second' closing.

Interesting points in this case ......

The exchange facilitator or intermediary was bypassed

The taxpayer already owned the land he wished to build on - you cannot exchange real property for an improvement made on another piece of real estate you already own

The taxpayer failed to transfer all of the benefits and burdens of ownership to the other party but by agreement retained those benefits and burdens.

Lesson in this case ....

Use an experienced Intermediary or Accommodator

A Great Scenario... Definitely not a court case....
At least not yet.....................

Dick and Jane are husband and wife. They own a home in California (only in California can this happen). They have owned the home for 12 years and it has $1,000,000 in Capital gain. They also own 2 rental properties each of which have more than $500,000. in Capital gain.

Dick and Jane are not happy and decide to divorce. In their divorce settlement, they agree to hold the family home and each will take one of the rental properties. Jane and her personal trainer marry and move into her rental property. They live there for two years and decide to sell the property. They as joint taxpayers claim the primary residence exclusion of $500,000. (joint) and move into the marital home.

Dick and the Aupair agree to marry. They live in the family home for 2 years and then move into the other rental property.

During the third year that Jane and her personal trainer are living in the family home, Dick and Jane decide to sell the property since the children are now in college. The property sold and each couple elected to exclude $500,000 of gain on the sale of a primary residence. They meet the exclusion requirements because each couple lived in the residence for two of the five years immediately prior to the sale and at least one member of each couple was an owner of the property for 2 of the 5 years immediately prior to sale.

Dick and his Aupair sell the other rental property 2 years later and they exclude $500,000 (joint) in capital gain on the sale of their primary residence.

So, with good planning these taxpayers managed to exclude $2,000,000 from taxation over a 7 year period.

Oddly enough, the new law regarding primary residences allow this. For how long remains to be seen...........?

Remember the DOs and DON'Ts

Happy Exchanging

About the Author

Bettye Matthews is a certified public accountant licensed in both Florida and Maryland. She first began her experience with 1031 tax deferred exchanges as an instructor with the Adult Education Division of the University of Maryland. In that capacity, she facilitated discussions regarding Real Estate Taxation which included descriptive formulas for deferring tax by using Internal Revenue Code Section 1031. At that time the "Safe Harbor" discussed in this handbook was not available and exchanges were a tedious and dangerous undertaking.

Mrs. Matthews is currently the President and CEO of Exchange Professionals, Inc. with offices in Naples, Florida and Westminster, Maryland. The company provides Qualified Intermediary and Accommodator services to real estate investors.

For lists of other Qualified Intermediaries throughout the country, check the web site of The Federation of Exchange Accommodators at www.1031.org.

Notes to
Self

And

Questions
to ask

Notes to
Self

And

Questions
to ask